OBSESSED V

(EXPLORING INTIM

DEDICATION

This book is dedicated to the most Holy and Magnificent God, my Heavenly Father Yahweh, The Great I AM. He is the one who has shown me so much love. His careful guidance and watchfulness over my life means more to me than I can say. I am so grateful that He chose me to be His adopted child. I dedicate my life to Him, and I am His humble servant for the rest of my life. I love you so, my Father God!

I would also like to dedicate this book to my husband Rev. James A. Nemley who compelled me for years to write this book. He has always been my cheer leader in everything that I do for the Lord. He has been with me through every step of this process for publishing this book. He is **TEAM TANYA** for sure. He is also my prayer partner and spiritual life partner. I love you!

My final dedication is to my Granddaughter, Olivia Grayce Merrick whose words "Grandma is obsessed with God", was such an inspiration to me. My prayer is that she will want to love God as a young child just like I did. Olivia I love you!

Chapters:

FORWARD

Olivia Grayce Merrick
Tanya's Granddaughter and inspiration for this book!

My grandmother is obsessed with the Lord. I know that because she prays for everyone, and she cares about the Lord. She takes religion seriously! She knows the Lord loves her. She teaches me about the Lord and how I can have a strong relationship with him. That is one of the reasons why I love my grandmother. Finally, she knows that the Lord will take care of her. Olivia Merrick 11 years old.

Rev. James A. Nemley, President
Living For The Kingdom Bible Ministry

When reading my wife's book, "Obsessed With God" you can't help but enter into His throne room! Have you ever wondered how other people seem to radiate when seeking God in prayer? Have you ever wondered how God responds to them? Do you desire to draw closer to the Lord? Then you MUST read, "Obsessed With God!"

Every chapter is written from God's throne room. Page by page you begin to understand how God should be loved and reverenced. Tanya takes you into her prayer closet and doesn't let you out until you fully understand what it is to be, "Obsessed With God!"

I have been with my wife for over 40 years and have seen her hunger and desire to get closer to God. There were times when I would come home from work to find her in tears, as I walked in during her private times of prayer. She would share with me the details of her time with God and I would share with her some scripture verses about what she had just experienced.

Over the years I have seen her through all her ups and downs, and I've seen the way God has blessed her through it all. Her victories from trials have drawn her so close to God. I am intimately aware of her unique relationship with the Lord. To say that she is, "Obsessed" with Him is an understatement!

When you look up the definition of obsessed you find a lot of negative information. Obsessed means to be; *preoccupied or to fill the mind of (someone) continually.* This is exactly what the Lord wants us to be! Obsessed!

When we wholeheartedly seek after God, we too can become obsessed. Read Tanya's book and learn how you too can become, "Obsessed With God!"

Samantha Tetro
Founder Samantha's "Li'l Bit of Heaven" Ministries

Searching for an easy to read book on acquiring a more intimate relationship with God? Look no further! In "Obsessed with God", author Tanya Nemley gently invites you into her life, her love and her Lord. Tanya is transparent in expressing the real and raw emotions of her faith journey. In addition, she also shares with you the prayers and secrets on how to obtain the very thing she spent her life looking for.

Her heartfelt cry throughout the pages of this book, is that all would know how loved they are by God. Mission Accomplished! This book can apply to both the seeker and the mature believer. It creates a hunger for what is an endless supply of HIS love. "Obsessed with God", is the little book with a life changing message!

Judge John Andrew Kay

Intimacy is defined as "close familiarity or friendship; closeness." My precious friend, Tanya Nemley, now takes us on a journey of intimacy which was forged in the pain of her personal uncertainty and insecurity. Only this time the destination of our intimacy will be with the Creator of the Universe and the Creator of you and me as Tanya shows us that our tears are the proof of His presence.

Tanya lovingly takes us where Isaiah was in 26:9, *"My soul yearns for You in the night, in the morning my spirit yearns for You."* She challenges us to believe that you and I are an intimate and indispensable part of His wonderful plan. You will see why

Tanya cries out that she "found God's amazing, deep, piercing, overflowing, comforting, fear removing, strengthening Love!"

As you turn the pages you are about to start on a journey and your guide is Tanya Nemley. As you read on you may think that she perhaps thinks of herself as an unlikely guide but you will discover, as I did, that God's hand guided her through the depths of the darkness of her life so that she could now become our beacon in the darkness of ours, shining all on the God she has become so rightly **OBSESSED** with.

The destination of this exciting journey is found in the arms of God Himself, now and forever; Tanya shows us how it is hers as she yearns for us to make it ours as well.

Forward by: Dr. Juliet S. Pinder- McBride
Co-Founder of McBride Ministries

You will not be able to put this book down until you are finished. Your life will be changed, transformed and restored! Rev. Tanya Nemley gives you detailed steps on how to have an intimate relationship with God. As you read each page you will learn and see through scriptures, and her personal experiences, how much God loves you. She gives you a glimpse of the "heart" of Abba Father and our relationship to Him.

You will learn how God created us to worship and fellowship with Him. Rev. Nemley challenges you to "cherish" the time you spend with the Father and the importance of communicating with Him. She is concise, reflective, and transparent about her insecurities and spiritual growth. The book propels you to take a "leap of faith" to fully commit your life to the Lord through intimacy. Matt 22:37 is the theme of this phenomenal book...... "Love the Lord your God with all your heart and with all your soul and with all your mind."

Alex Valentino
Song Writer & Recording Artist

"To know this author personally, is to know and confirm the pages of her book, "Obsessed With God." Tanya Nemley, whether she is sharing her testimony, ministering in song, or she is telling a personal story, bears a testimony to the Christian experience - both on the mountains and in the valleys of life. Gods' blessings have truly led her to become "Obsessed With God."

Bobby Riedel, Pastor
Sound of Heaven Church

Tanya Nemley is no stranger to the things of God! She has been saved since 12 years old, and has a plethora of experience with the Lord. Maybe that's why she's "Obsessed With God"! From The highs to the lows, and everywhere in between, Tanya's intimacy with the Lord increased.

What I love about this read is the simplicity of it. The one thing that stands out to me is Tanya's child-like approach in her relationship with Him. We should all have this! Tanya is so innocent and real in her love of Abba Father, that it truly reminds me of how transparent children are when they are captivated by things in their own world. This child-like zeal for the Lord, grew overtime. Her prayer life alone is an indication of that! Wait till you read that journey!

The word says in Matthew 18: 1-5, "At that time the disciples came to Jesus and asked, "Who, then, is the greatest in the kingdom of heaven?"

2. He called a little child to him, and placed the child among them. 3. And he said: "Truly I tell you, unless you change and become like little children, you will never enter the kingdom of heaven. 4. Therefore, whoever takes the lowly position of this child is the greatest in the kingdom of heaven. 5. And whoever welcomes one such child in my name welcomes me.
Tanya, to me, is the epitome of this! Let her personal stories encourage you to find the child in you again. May her journey prompt you to begin again. It's never too late. Nothing separates us from the love of God. No sin, struggle, or shortcoming...maybe that's why one of Tanya's favorite songs to sing is, "Jesus Loves Me". After all, we are His children.

Don't let your years in Christianity prevent you from reading this masterpiece! I dare you to read...let the words penetrate your spirit.

INTRODUCTION

I decided to write this book because of something my granddaughter said about me. She told her mother that "grandma is obsessed with God." When I found out her opinion of me, I said, "Praise God! She gets me!" I must admit, though, that I am obsessed with God. Her statement really opened my eyes to understand how I feel about God. This has been such a revelation to me about myself.

Obsessed means to constantly think about something, to dwell on that thing, and to be preoccupied with it. Obsessed kind of has a negative tone to it, so I guess I would prefer maybe saying that "I'm really into the Lord!"

Why am I obsessed? Because God loves me for who I am. Warts and all. He healed me from major clinical depression and suicidal ideation. He also, over the years since I became a committed Christian, has performed many miracles in my life and has answered many of my prayers, which have continued to feed into my obsession with God.

My obsession with God is that I eat, sleep, talk about and breathe Jesus 24 hours a day, seven days a week. He's all that I want to think about and talk about.

Isaiah 26:9 says, *"My soul yearns for you in the night; in the morning my spirit longs for you." (NIV)*

The subtitle for my book is ***INTIMACY WITH GOD***, which means the closeness one feels in a relationship. It's *sharing your personal thoughts and feelings with another person that you truly trust.* It's *being emotionally involved with that person.* Intimacy can be with close friends, family, a boyfriend or in a marriage. In this case, we are talking about having a *very close* relationship with God! There is a song that I love by a terrific songwriter named Thomas Whitfield. The song is entitled, "Wrapped up, Tied up, Tangled up in Jesus." It's an unusual name for a song, but it's the anthem of my life!

Jesus Himself told us to love God with everything that we are and from the depths of the heart. When I read this, I was like, "Ok, Jesus, I will surely try to do that!" and ever since then, I have been on a mission to becoming **OBSESSED WITH GOD**. The following scripture verse has been my main motivation for obtaining my passion:

Matthew 22:37, Jesus replied: *"Love the Lord your God with all your heart and with all your soul and with all your mind.'* (NIV) In Deuteronomy 6:5, it uses the words, *with all your strength.* I love that word strength in reference to loving God. To me, it means to exert *every bit of effort and energy* into being 100% involved with God all day, every single day, until the day He takes you home to heaven! Now, this doesn't mean that you have no earthly life at all. It means that you need to make sure that God is *front and center* in your life and in everything that you do. Throughout the pages of this book, I hope to take you through my journey of discovery about God that has led me to my obsession with Him. First, I want to talk about some facts about the uniqueness about God, like how *mysterious* He is, *where* His love for us started, the *wonderful plans* He has for us, and *why* He loves us. I've also included some of my most personal prayer secrets!

What I experienced in prayer doesn't make me extra special because God doesn't play favorites with His children. We are all special to God, and He will reveal Himself to anyone who wants to fellowship with Him.

I ask that as you read this book that you will keep an open mind and open your heart to desiring a deeper walk with our Father God. My hope is that you will see that God is a very hands-on and interactive Father who wants to be **so involved** with you. He never meant for you to feel alone in this world. God uniquely made a way for Himself to contact you and for you to contact Him, whenever and how often you want to.

There was a movie that came out in 2009 called, *"He's Just Not That Into you."* Well, a movie should come out called, *"He's just so into you!"* This is how I feel about my relationship with God.

God is *into us,* and when you figure this out, you will be so obsessed with Him too!

1 John 4:19 says, *"We love him because he first loved us."* (NIV)

When I became a committed Christian, I told God to take me as far with Him that I can humanly go. It's been like diving off a high building straight into His loving arms! It's like seeing myself sitting on His lap and Him holding me like the loving Father that He is. I've had some very difficult times in my life and my obsession with God has helped me hold steady through it all. I know that God loves me and has the best motives for my life. All the love that I have ever needed God has it available for me. My relationship with God has been such an incredible blessing to me that I'm hoping others can glean something from my experiences. I hope, through the pages of this book, you might also begin to become "obsessed with God too!"

CHAPTER 1

THE MYSTERIOUSNESS OF GOD

Job 11:7-8 (MSG) *"Do you think you can explain the mystery of God? Do you think you can diagram God Almighty? God is far higher than you can imagine, far deeper than you can comprehend."*

God is extremely unique, and He is surely a mystery to mankind. He is the *Almighty, all-knowing, all-powerful God!* God is a supreme being! He is the highest and greatest power and authority over all things! There is nothing over God, and He says this about Himself, *"I Am Who I Am!"* There's nothing really left to say after this statement. God has chosen to give us a certain amount of information about Himself, and after that, nothing! Whatever the bible says about Him, whatever this earth reveals about Him and whatever the Holy Spirit confirms to us about Him, that is all we get! I also think that If we knew everything about God right now, we would see Him as a regular person, or maybe we might become too familiar with Him. That could be why He hasn't told us everything about Himself.

God is so much more! I do respect His privacy about Himself. I believe He concealed this information for our benefit. Have you ever heard of the term TMI, too much information? We would be consumed by the vastness of this information, and we would not be able to process all of it. We have trouble now just trying to understand the Trinity of the Godhead.

Colossians 2:2-3 says, *"That their hearts might be comforted, being knit together in love, and unto all riches of the full assurance of understanding, to the acknowledgement of the mystery of God, and of the Father, and of Christ; 3 In whom are hid all the treasures of wisdom and knowledge."* (NIV)

Before the creation of earth, there was a whole universe existing and heavenly activities going on. Can you try to imagine what God was doing? I know, difficult isn't it? We have nothing in our minds that we can base any logical thoughts on this subject—nothing to compare it to in our sphere of knowledge. The mystery of God does greatly increase my curiosity about Him. I want to know so much more about His Majesty and Glory. I do know from His own description about Himself that His power is *out of this world and unexplainable!* This knowledge about God feeds more into my obsession with Him and causes me to think about Him with wonder, awe, and fear.

There are no human thoughts or words to even try to describe who He really is. I'm drawn to search the scriptures so that I can try to wrap my mind around this great mystery. I try to assimilate the bible's limited amount of information that God has allowed us to know about Himself. I'm so excited to know that my Father God is uniquely set apart from anything that we have ever known. He is supernatural, all-knowing and is an all-powerful being who

> *There are no human thoughts or words to even try to describe who He really is.*

has always been in existence and is eternal.

I've been searching to know more of God most of my life. *I just can't get enough of Him,* so I keep digging and searching for more information. Sometimes in prayer, He gives me a gift of experiencing His Shekinah Glory! In other words, His presence, but this just makes me hungrier for Him!

Not knowing everything about God might have some advantages. *FIRST,* we would be scared to death of Him because we would know the fullness of His holiness and suffer from knowing our own sinfulness in comparison. *SECOND,* we would get used to Him or become too familiar with Him. He might not be as special to us anymore. Look at how people have become too familiar with Him now.

Jesus's heavenly life is a mystery also, but the reason for His earthly appearance has been revealed to us. Luke 4:43 say, *"But he said, "I must proclaim the good news of the kingdom of God to the other towns also because that is why I was sent."* (NIV).

God's whole existence is so fascinating to me! I like to meditate on who He is from my research about Him from the bible. From my research, I do know that God is a spirit being, and He is unlike anyone or anything we have ever known! As powerful and Holy as He is, He sent His only Son to come down here and humble Himself to ensure that we had a way back to Him! Heaven is truly our real home!

So, for right now, I will spend as much time as I can in God's presence through prayer. I will also rely on the Holy Spirit's ability to help me experience God in an intimate way. I will scour the scriptures to expose all available information about God the Father, God the Son and God the Holy Spirit so that I can continually be in awe of *His MYSTERIOUSNESS!*

Even through His awesome power, holiness, and majesty, He has made a way for us to connect with Him until we can finally see Him face to face! Oh, **I'M SO OBSESSED WITH MY GOD!**

CHAPTER 2

THE CHALLENGE TO LOVE AN INVISIBLE GOD

Colossians 1:15 says, *"The Son is the image of the invisible God, the firstborn over all creation."* (NIV)

Is it hard to be in love with God who is invisible? Yes and no. Yes, because we have never seen His face. People fall in love with people they have met online, so we know that it is possible to love someone without seeing them physically. But to develop something that leads to a real relationship and eventually, marriage, you must see them face to face. No, because we have the bible and the confirmation from the Holy Spirit who lives inside of us when we accepted Jesus as our Savior.

> *Is it hard to be in love with God who is invisible?*

We can never physically see God in our present human form. Exodus 33:20 says, *"But," he said, "you cannot see my face, for no one may see me and live."* (NIV) So how can we have this relationship with our supernatural God? My hope is that as you continue to read this book about my personal experiences with God, you will come to understand that this is possible. It does take time, patience, and a willingness to achieve this.

Your acceptance of Jesus Christ as your Lord and Savior was the first big step. Your relationship with Jesus will reveal Father God to you because Jesus has seen and knows God from a human perspective, and Jesus is God.

John 1:18 says, *"No one has ever seen God, but the one and only Son, who is Himself God and is in closest relationship with the Father, has made Him known."* (NIV)

I try not to form any kind of picture of what I think God's face may look like. I know that seeing His face is a special thing that will be shown to me on that special day when I get to heaven. So, for right now, I will try to see Him through scripture, through prayer and through admiring and meditating on His attributes. Some people imagine God to look like an old man with gray hair and a long white beard. When I think of God, I picture Him in my mind on His throne because of this glorious description of Him from the prophet Ezekiel in the bible.

Ezekiel 10:4 says, *"Then the glory of the LORD rose from above the cherubim and moved to the threshold of the temple. The cloud filled the temple, and the court was full of the radiance of the glory of the LORD."* (NIV)

Someone painted a picture of what they thought Jesus looked like, and over the years, people have run with that. It's a little strange to not be able to see our Father God, but don't let that hinder your relationship with Him. God is in us, and because of this fact, we can know God very intimately without ever seeing His face. We can also experience God supernaturally in ways that I will share about in how I accomplished this throughout this book.

1 Corinthians 3:16 says, *"Do you not know that you yourselves are God's temple, and that God's Spirit dwells in you?"* (NIV)

CHAPTER 3

IN THE BEGINNING

2 Timothy 1:9 says, *"He has saved us and called us to a holy life--not because of anything we have done but because of His own purpose and grace. This grace was given us in Christ Jesus before the beginning of time."*

Human life may have physically started at the creation of mankind, but God had a plan for man *way before* then. There was a plan put in place for God's only Son Jesus Christ to rescue us *before the beginning of time* and the creation of earth. Because of God's love and grace, you and I are a part of His wonderful plan.

> *There was a plan put in place for*
> *God's only Son Jesus Christ to rescue*
> *us before the beginning of time and*
> *the creation of earth.*

But, why should the most *powerful, majestic,* and *holy* being in the entire universe love us lowly, sinful, little Rugrats? A rugrat is a small child who is learning to get around by crawling and eventually walking on their own. They are very short on social skills and are trying to grow and develop. They are rude, whinny and very temperamental and sometimes straight-up bad! With time and good training, they can mature and become a great asset to society. I hope you're not insulted that I called us a rugrat, but we are like young children to God, and we need to spiritually *grow up* and *mature.* We are created beings who sinned from our very beginning. The first humans, Adam & Eve, were very disobedient and wound up doing things that were not pleasing to the Lord. Yes, we all are sinners and fall far short of the holiness of God. But as bad and as flawed as we are, our Creator has an *incredible* amount of love for us!!! He surely doesn't have to love us. So, why does He?

If you see God and His creations as the beginning in the first chapter of Genesis, you will not get the whole picture about just how much God loves you. His love for us did not start with creation. God's beginning for each person's life started in God's mind! This is where the thought of our existence was first conceived by God's love. God loved you before any of this thing called creation even came about. We are not the after effect of 2 humans uniting and making a baby. Nobody's life is unplanned or unexpected. Nobody is a mistake or happened by accident.

Romans 8:29 says, *"For those God foreknew he also predestined to be conformed to the image of His Son, that He might be the firstborn among many brothers and sisters."* (NIV)

Satan tries to get you to believe the lie that you're a nobody. He even tries to get you to believe in evolution or that there is no God so he can cover up God's love for you. This is one of Satan's greatest deceptions. The devil tries to get you to believe that God doesn't love you. The devil uses all of the struggles and turmoil in your life to try to convince you that God has forgotten about you. And then he whispers in your ear that God can't possibly love you. It's all lies! I tell you it's a lie!

Have we been a victim of Satan's lies? Every year millions of kids are told a big lie that there's a man named Santa Claus who will bring them lots of toys. And let's not forget about the tooth fairy and the Easter bunny! Not only did we believe it ourselves, *but we fed this lie to our very own children!* We are adults now, and although we were manipulated to believe these lies, we know the truth now, and no one can ever get us to start believing in Santa Claus again! Well, the devil fed us all a pack of lies our whole lives, that we are so sinful to ever be accepted by God. We know the truth now, but let's get the whole truth, which is *just how much* God loves us and why He loves us so. Ephesians 1:4 says, *"For He chose us in Him BEFORE the creation of the world to be holy and blameless in His sight."* (NIV)

Jeremiah 29:11 says, *"For I know the plans I have for you,"* declares the LORD, *"plans to prosper you and not to harm you, plans to give you hope and a future."*

So, you see, God had plans for you all along. These are *good* plans too. One day while in my deep prayer closet time with the Lord, I asked Him why did He create us? Then God asked me why I wanted children. I told Him that I wanted someone to love that was a part of me and He said to me, that's why I wanted children, I wanted someone to love that was a part of me."

Isaiah 43:7 says, *"Everyone who is called by My name, whom I created for My glory, whom I formed and made."* (NIV)

I think that God has probably created many different galaxies and other beings. But I think that creating someone and coming up with a plan to redeem them and then calling them Your children has made us all *very special* to God. I believe God has the deepest supernatural love for us!

1 John 4:9-10 says, *"This is how God showed His love among us: He sent His one and only Son into the world that we might live through Him. This is love: not that we loved God, but that He loved us and sent His Son as an atoning sacrifice for our sins."* (NIV)

God is also emotionally connected to us. He sent His only Son Jesus to earth to sacrifice Himself for our sins so that we can have eternal life. Since Jesus is God the Son, He let the beings that He created torture Him and then murder Him. Now that is love! God then puts the 3rd person of the Trinity (still Himself), God the Holy Spirit, inside the bodies of His children. This is so that He can be in constant communication with them and help them know Him personally. If that ain't love, *I just don't know what is!!!!* One of the greatest blessings for us is that we will never suffer any pain or agony ever again! Jesus has prepared a great home for us to live in with Father God, and we will reign and rule with Him forever!!!

Revelations 21:4 says, *"He will wipe EVERY tear from their eyes. There will be no more death' or mourning or crying or pain, for the old order of things has passed away."* (NIV)

I never thought that anyone could love me this much! At first, I didn't know how to receive God's love for me. I had been programmed my whole life to be in an extremely low self-worth mode to the point of trying to commit suicide. I didn't even let my husband love me back. I just thought I was not worthy of that kind of love. But over time, I began to feel the power of God's love for me, and even my husband's love for me. The more I learned God's word, the more I began to understand why God had created me in the first place, and this made me feel very special. I now go around saying to myself, *"I'M GOD'S GIRL!"* I know this very well now!

Psalm 139:13 -14 says, *"For you created my inmost being; you knit me together in my mother's womb. I praise you because I am fearfully and wonderfully made; Your works are wonderful; I know that full well."* (NIV)

God even reassures us that nothing will ever remove His love for us. Romans 8:37-39 says, *"For I am convinced that neither death, nor life, nor angels, nor principalities, nor things present, nor things to come, nor powers, nor height, nor depth, nor any other created thing, will be able to separate us from the love of God, which is in Christ Jesus our Lord."* (NIV). Now, this is some *deep* love. We don't even always behave! You know we must get on God's nerves sometimes, but nothing will ever *separate us* from His love! Thank God Jesus and the Holy Spirit are always working to help us to live a holy life in preparation to be presented to God one day. God thought of everything in His plan for our lives!

This scripture verse makes me just want to cry for joy. Romans 5:8 say, *"But God demonstrates His own love for us in this: While we were still sinners, Christ died for us."* (NIV). Jesus's death on the cross was a demonstration of God's love for me! Not only did He love me, *but He did something to prove it! JESUS SAVED*

ME FROM EVER EXPERIENCING THE WRATH OF GOD! NOW THAT IS POWERFUL!!!

This is what makes me want to get on my face before the throne of God and *kiss His feet* for the rest of my life. Sometimes I just randomly start crying because *I'm overwhelmed* that God loves me!

God loves me because He is love! Love is one of His attributes, as stated in the bible. 1 John 4:8 says, *"Whoever does not love does not know God, because God is love."* (NIV). *GOD IS LOVE*, and when I die, I'm going to experience the incredible fullness of God's love for me! I feel a microscopic amount of this now, but can you imagine feeling 100% of God's love?

I really hope you meditate on the love that God has for you. I feel this is so important in a Christian's life, and I hope this information gets you to be **OBSESSED WITH GOD** and can motivate you to make your life a living sacrifice to God for His kingdom.

Ephesians 2:4-5 says, *"But because of His great love for us, God, who is rich in mercy, made us alive with Christ even when we were dead in transgressions–it is by grace you have been saved."* (NIV). And this was all planned *BEFORE THE BEGINNING OF TIME!*

CHAPTER 4

GOD'S INTIMATE CREATION

OF MAN

Psalms 139:14 says, *"I praise you because I am fearfully and wonderfully made; Your works are wonderful, I know that full well."* (NIV)

When God created man, He formed him in a very unique and intimate way. He could have just thought of man and poof, he became a human. But God personally wanted to be more *hands-on* and *physically* involved in the job of creating the first human. The first unique thing He did was to make a man and a woman in His image. The bible says God is spirit, so we are made up of spirit too.

> **When God created man, He formed him in a very unique and intimate way.**

Genesis 1:7 says, *"So God created mankind in His own image, in the image of God He created them; male and female He created them."* (NIV)

The second thing that God did was to gather up some dust from the ground and formed Adam's body.

The third thing that happened is God blew His very own breath into Adam's body to make Adam come alive!

Genesis 2:7 says, *"Then the LORD God formed a man from the dust of the ground and breathed into his nostrils the breath of life, and the man became a living being."* (NIV)

So, you see that our relationship With God is much more intimate because He was *personally involved* in creating us. Much involvement and thought went into our creation, so we can see that we were not just created on a whim. What an *incredibly close relationship* we have with our Maker!

We were carefully thought of and put together by God Himself. He didn't do this from His throne, but He actually came down to earth to accomplish this! What I can glean from this small amount of information about our creation and development is this gives us some insight into God's heart and mind. It shows us that He was sentimental in the way that He wanted to create us by *doing it* Himself. To me, this really proves not only how much He is invested in us, but most of all, it proves how much He loves us. In this book, we are going to examine the ways that God not only designed our bodies but how He made it so that He could also live in us. Like the caring Father that He is, He has been very protective of us. He has given us the Holy Spirit, who lives in us, and He has even provided angels to watch over us. If this doesn't show His deepest love for His creations, I don't know what does!

CHAPTER 5

ARE WE REALLY ONE WITH GOD?

1 Corinthians 6:17 says, *"But whoever is united with the Lord is one with Him in spirit."* (NIV)

We need to be very faithful in our relationship with God because we are actually one with Him. I want you to meditate on the fact that *WE ARE ONE WITH GOD.* God is a spirit, and we have a spirit contained in our physical body. That's what makes it possible for us to have this unique and intimate relationship with God. When we accepted Jesus as our Lord and Savior, *WE BECAME ONE WITH GOD.* Our bodies became *THE TEMPLE OF THE HOLY SPIRIT!*

> **When we accepted Jesus as our Lord and Savior, WE BECAME ONE WITH GOD.**

1 Corinthians 6:19 says, *"Do you not know that your bodies are temples of the Holy Spirit, who is in you, whom you have received from God? You are not your own."* (NIV)

This is a symbiotic relation that we have with our Father God. In other words, we are *two living spirit beings who are connected and interacting with one another* but who are also different in nature. We exist in two different realms. Also, God is spirit, and we are human. We are dependent on God, and He is always there for us.

John 14:20-21 says, *"On that day you will realize that I am in My Father, and you are in Me, and I am in you."* (NIV)

It's a very special relationship that those who are not Christians can't understand, and those who are Christians may not fully comprehend. That's why I've included this chapter in this book. I find that some people really have difficulty believing that God loves them, and this may be the reason they can't go very deep in their relationship with God. How can you feel love from a person who you think allows you to needlessly suffer? How can you develop a passionate relationship with someone who you don't feel really loves you?

> *How can you feel love from a person*
> *who you think allows you to*
> *needlessly suffer?*

How do you picture yourself in your relationship with God? Do you keep Him at a distance? Is He someone you visit when you go to church? Is He just in the pages of your bible when you read it? Have you made Him personal in your life? Well, He resides with you in your body. It's you, God the Father, God the Son and God the Holy Spirit living inside of you. He is as close as someone could be to you.

For me, this knowledge has been responsible for my obsession with God. I feel like knowing that God is in me, and I am in God has put me over the top with feeling connected to my God.

I meditate on scripture verses that reveal God to me so that I can know more about God and feel closer to Him mentally, emotionally and spiritually! We cannot connect to God physically because He is a spirit being, but we can connect with Him in every other way because of the Holy Spirit living inside of us. I will be sharing with you in the upcoming chapters of this book the unique ways in which I connect with God.

CHAPTER 6

OUR LOVE CONNECTION

WITH GOD

1 John 4:8 says, *"Whoever does not love does not know God, because God is love."* (NIV)

Because of this scripture, I know that I need to live right. I need to be Holy! I need to repent when I do wrong. I don't want to shame my Father God! He knows about everything I do and say. I need to live a life that's pleasing to the Lord. No wonder King David prayed the following prayer:

Psalms 51:9-10 says, *"Hide your face from my sins and blot out all my iniquity. Create in me a pure heart, O God, and renew a steadfast spirit within me."* (NIV)

> *A part of being obsessed with God is making sure my heart stays clean.*

A part of being obsessed with God is making sure my heart stays clean. Being sinful is a problem if I want to be close with God. I cannot get close to God with a dirty, sinful heart. I need to repent and ask for forgiveness because of God's holiness. If I am to have this deep connection with God, I need to have a clean heart. I do miss the mark because I'm human but thank God for the guidance and conviction of the Holy Spirit to keep me on track.

I need purity in my life. I need to live a holy life because I need my relationship with God to be pleasing to Him so that I can keep the lines of communication open with Him. This means I need to be in a right relationship with God and be loving and kind with those around me such as family, friends and acquaintances. I don't want anything that could possibly impede my prayer life.

To stay in this close love relationship with God, we also need to obey God. The scriptures say that God commands us to do so.

This will let God know that we indeed love Him, and God will surely reward us by showing Himself to us.

John 14:21 says, *"Whoever has My commands and keeps them is the one who loves Me. The one who loves Me will be loved by My Father, and I too will love them and show Myself to them."* (NIV)

CHAPTER 7

GOD REALLY DOES LOVE YOU!

1 John 4:19 says, *"We love Him, because He first loved us."* (NIV)

There was a time in my life that I didn't know how much God loved me. I wasn't sure of His love for me at all. I couldn't see it and I couldn't feel it. One day when I was praying, I was really feeling God's love for me. I asked myself "how do I really know that God really loves me?"

Of course, we know because the bible tells us that He loved us first! But His love goes way deeper than that.

The first reason that I know God loves me is because the more that I have studied about God and I discovered who He really is, the more that knowledge, the reason for His love for me became real in my spirit and revealed biblical truth to me!!!!! The power of the Holy Spirit supernaturally confirmed this directly to me!! God has a supernatural way of communicating with His children so that they are reassured of His existence and of His love and care for them.

So, for me, the more knowledge that I get about God, the more I feel His love and why He had Jesus sacrifice His life for me!

The second reason that I know God loves me is because of all the past miracles He has done for me and for the many victories he's given me. If I am a Christian and I don't know how much God loves me, this will cause me to stumble and fall. I will be a weak Christian! I will also doubt Gods' abilities to see me safely through every circumstance in my life.

If we don't understand just how much God loves us...nothing about God will make any sense! We will always be very fearful during hard trials and lose hope and will often become discouraged. We'll experience a lot of doubt and could lose our faith. We may frequently be mad at God and blame Him for any calamities or sudden disasters.

From a very early age, I never knew what love was. I felt that nobody loved me. I had never felt it. Because of this, I didn't know what real love was, and I couldn't interpret or even respond

> *If we don't understand just how much God loves us...nothing about God will make any sense!*

to it. Since it was never available to me, it caused me a great deal of grief in my life and affected my personality. By the time I was about 12, I tried to commit suicide. I thought of suicide very often because of feeling lonely and hopeless. I did learn about God as a child and took great comfort in talking to God often, but I didn't receive God's love in my heart because I didn't know how to respond to Him that way.

When I turned 18, I gave myself away needlessly looking for someone to say that they loved me. Even if they had said that to me, I wouldn't have believed them. That was because I never knew how to receive love, and I thought I was an unlovable mistake. I didn't think I was special to God or anyone else.

My first marriage didn't go well, so, for me, this was confirmation that I was unlovable! Sometime later, I married again, and this time to a man who was very loving, and for two-thirds of my marriage, I didn't think my husband really loved me. I told him he was just co-dependent on me. I was damaged goods! No real emotions came from me. I couldn't even express love in a regular or normal way!

I didn't think God could love someone like me. I felt like I kept failing Him and disappointing Him. God tried to show me and tell me that He loved me, but I just could not accept it. My husband also tried to convince me of this to no avail. I didn't even feel human. Maybe I was really a robot, an artificial life form. I was like Data the android on the Star Trek TV. I had no emotions at all!

I wish I could say that there was a big ah-ha moment when I realized that God really loved me, but it has been a process. As I began to seek help for my issues with love, I found my answers in God's word, and through a great deal of talking with God.

I can now say with 100% certainty that my husband really loves me from the depths of his heart!!! I know it for sure! I have learned my own love language, and since I'm not the greatest at verbally expressing love, I've learned how to love in my own way. I know now how to express my love and emotions to my husband and to others.

I'm sharing this very personal information about myself for the purpose of getting you to see how much God loves you and what He did for me and why I'm obsessed with Him.

For many reasons, some of which I just shared with you, I could not accept God's love for me. I thought He was so disappointed with me that He was trying to squish me like a bug. I felt that He was always punishing me. But I finally have realized that *GOD REALLY LOVES ME AND ALWAYS HAS AND ALWAYS WILL!!!!!!* God showed me how I was conceived in His heart and mind and that His love for me was always there. I was thought of and born out of His love for me. But once I left God's mind and came through the universe and down into my mom's womb, my perfect life changed because of original sin caused by Adam and Eve.

So now, I had to go through the process in my life to get put back right with God. I needed to be in a right relationship with Him. He already loved me so much, but I needed to get to learn how to love Him. I really needed to fall in love with God. It was difficult because of all the emotional baggage I had. I associated my suffering with God's love for me. I would say, "How can God really love me and let me go through all this pain?" I had to separate all my suffering away from my love for God. I needed to take a page from Job and say, Job 13:15 says, *"Though He slay me, yet will I trust in Him."* (NIV). I had to learn to sing this well-known hymn and mean it, *"It is well with my soul."* I had to learn to love God despite all the things that might be going on in my life. I had to learn that God loves me no matter what I do or don't do.

Everybody wants to be loved. It's a fact! We first look for love from our parents and then from other people. We instinctively seem to need it. God made us like that! We know we need love, but what can we do about it? God's love was always there! We thought that human relationships would satisfy us fully. Human love is good but not perfect and will occasionally let us down. We need a steady, fulfilling, and complete love, so we keep searching. I was searching everywhere, and then I hit the jackpot! I found God's amazingly deep, piercing, overflowing, comforting, fear removing, strengthening love! His love is mind-blowing!

I get teary-eyed and emotional every time I think about how much God loves me. You might ask me this question; how do I know that God loves me? This is my answer, one day when I was thinking about how hard my life was, God showed me my whole life like a movie playing in my mind. He showed all the times that He bought me through my heavy trials and all the near-missed car accidents for my family. He showed how He brought 4 of my children back from the brink of death because they were all born prematurely. I cried so hard when He showed me this. One of my children was born not breathing, and I begged God in those moments after her birth to save her life, and He did. When my son was born and had a massive brain hemorrhage, I was told that he would never walk or talk. I begged God to heal Him, and He did. God has done many miracles for me, and I know He loves me.

The bible is filled with God's love for me. The more I study the bible, the more that I'm assured of this. The more that I pray and interact with God the Father, God the Son and God the Holy Spirit, the more I know that God loves me.

I think the more we understand about how much God loves us, the more we can comprehend this: *God had a plan to create us, Satan has a plan to destroy us and Jesus had a plan to redeem us!* God had plans to make us in His own image and to love us before Satan was ever created. God's plan was to have more children in addition to His one and only Son, Jesus, so He made us and made a way for us to become adopted into His family.

If you don't realize how much Jesus loves you, then you have no foundation for the purpose of your life. You'll just keep searching for your purpose, and you might end up getting into some situations that aren't good for you.

What else could God possibly do for you when He Himself came down here and laid down His own life for you? Who would do that?

Because I have finally figured out how much God loves me, I've decided to commit the rest of my life to Him. I've offered my life and my body as a living sacrifice to God because it's all that I have to offer Him. When somebody loves you so much, it makes you want to do anything you can for them. God's love for me consumes my thoughts day and night. Love can make you do that. My love for God is like this, when I first met my husband, we were so in love. Then during the first year of marriage, called the honeymoon period, love is very exciting and passionate. My love for God is intense all day every day now, and it keeps growing stronger.

I suffer from chronic illnesses, and I have constant trials going on. So how can it be that with all the difficulties in my life that I'm becoming deeper in love with God? It's because we have developed a close intimate relationship. I walk with God constantly. I've learned to pray without ceasing. I know that God has perfect love for me. I trust that God has my best interests in mind.

I want every person reading this to think about this question, *how close is your relationship to God?* Is it personal and intimate? Loving God is a full-time commitment that I hope can lead you into becoming obsessed with God. In the next chapter, I want to help you deepen your relationship with God by getting to know Him even more.

CHAPTER 8

DON'T HOLD SUFFERING

AGAINST GOD

I wanted to include this topic in my book because when we go through hardships, pain, and suffering, we may have difficulty sustaining a high level of love towards God. We may feel hurt, angry, and disappointed that God has allowed us to suffer or that He didn't answer our prayers the way we wanted Him to. This is because we sometimes equate suffering with God's love toward us. This could be a big stumbling block that can get in the way of our intimacy with God.

There are three really good scriptures that help put suffering into perspective.

John 16:33 says, *"I have told you these things, so that in me you may have peace. In this world you will have trouble. But take heart! I have overcome the world."* (NIV)

Proverbs 3:5 says, *"Trust in the LORD with all your heart and lean not on your own understanding;"* (NIV)

1 Corinthians 13:12 says, *"For now we see only a reflection as in a mirror; then we shall see face to face. Now I know in part; then I shall know fully, even as I am fully known."* (NIV)

I'm going to give you a quick biblical synopsis on suffering here. Jesus told us that we will have trouble in John 16:33. We are told to try not to understand the way God does things. We understand very little of God's ways, but one day, we will fully understand why God did what He did.

You see, when you know and understand how much God really loves you, you won't be affected by life's natural daily struggles. This is why Job said, Job 13:15 *"Though he slay me, yet will I trust in him: but I will maintain mine own ways before him."* (NIV) He couldn't have dealt with such tragedy if he wasn't sure of God's love for him.

A good example of this is I have a friend whose young husband died. I asked her was she struggling with anger towards God because of her husband's sudden death. She said, "oh no, God did not kill my husband. He is loving and kind and would never do that to me. The devil is responsible for his death." She didn't let her love of God be confused with what happened to her husband.

I was blown away by her answer because when something terrible happens to some people, or they read about a horrific tragedy in the news, the first thing they want to do is to blame God! They say, "what kind of loving God would do something like that?" Love God just because of who He is. Don't judge Him or His ways. Just love Him, period!

This is my thoughts on the matter of life's difficulties. *"It's God's world and God's ways!* He created this world and has all rights to it and us!

We must love God. Just love Him, period! We need to let our love for God stand on its own. One of God's greatest attributes

"It's God's world and God's ways!

is His love for us. Don't look at God in view of our troubles. That will cause us to judge and question Him and ask, "why God why?" 1 Peter 4:12 says, *"Dear friends, do not be surprised at the fiery ordeal that has come on you to test you, as though something strange were happening to you."* (NIV)

God is not springing anything on us. He warned us in His word that things will be challenging for us. Jesus did a lot for us so that we can succeed in this world. John 16:33 says, *"I have told you these things so that in me you may have peace. In this world, you will have trouble. But take heart! I have overcome the world."* (NIV). Yes, there is going to be trouble.

So, I thank the Lord for all that He's done for me. I pray when I need help, and I trust Him. I accept the grace He has offered me to get through everything I might go through. I'm also grateful for the comforter. If I don't keep this kind of attitude for my life, I will become very discouraged.

I absolutely don't need anger, doubt and disappointment to dampen my relationship with God. So, I know that I need to keep my trials and any suffering that I go through separate from my feelings towards God. I need to love Him all the time just because He is God my Father. I don't need to hold the difficulties in my life against Him. I know my Father God has my best interest at heart. This is very important for me to keep in mind if I want to continue to be obsessed with God. God has written out the whole plan for my life from beginning to end in the bible. It's His world and His way. Let's jump on His bandwagon! Let's not let anything stand in the way of our intimacy with God.

CHAPTER 9

HOW TO LOVE GOD

You might say, "What? Fall in love with God, you should just love Him." I will tell you that for me, it has been a process. I had to first accept Jesus as my Lord and Savior, find out about God, and then talk to Him. I also had to have the desire to love God with everything I am.

Psalms 18:1 says, *"I will love you, O LORD, my strength."* (KJV)

The word "will" in this scripture is interesting because the meaning of will is intent. You have got to want or desire to love God. Do you have it in your heart to actively be pursuing a love relationship with God? I Love the Lord, but I also have come to realize that my love for God must develop deep in my heart, and it needs to grow. God's love for us doesn't grow because He already loves us to the fullest extent. Because of our humanity, our relationships need to be nurtured to grow. Our relationship with God is no different. As we continue to interact with God, our love relationship towards Him will grow and get stronger.

> **You have got to want or desire to love God.**

A closer and deeper walk with God is the motivational force behind my desire to love God intimately, which in turn causes me to be obsessed with God. I desire to love God more; I want to, and I intend to!

I love the Lord so very much, and I have Him on my mind all the time every day. The Holy Spirit is always reassuring me how much God loves me. One of the first church songs I learned as a little child went like this, "Jesus loves me this I know, for the bible tells me so."

John 3:16 says, *"For God so loved the world that he gave his one and only Son, that whoever believes in Him shall not perish but have eternal life."* (NIV)

One day someone told you and I about God and His love for us. In my life, my parents were the first people to tell me about God. It has been up to me, though, to accept this love, accept Jesus Christ as my Savior, repent from my sin and believe in Him.

So, how does one fall in love with God? Here are some of my tips:

1. You should pray and talk to God as much as you can.
2. You should know all that you can about God. This can be accomplished by reading and studying your bible.
3. You should understand the reason why Jesus came to earth. What He did for you will increase your feelings about God. Meditate on Jesus's sacrifice for your eternal life often. The more you think about God's plan for you to be with Him forever, the more deeply you will fall in love with Him.
4. Don't hold the negative things that happened to you against God because this can affect your love connection with God.
5. Time will help you love God more. Give it time for your love feeling for Him to develop.
6. Surrender yourself 100% to Him. For example, when I married my husband, I made a commitment to Him. When you surrender yourself to the Lord, you make a commitment to Him. It's an ongoing relationship that needs to be nurtured every single day. Not just on Sunday, Easter and Christmas or when you have a need. It takes dedication on our part to maintain this relationship on a level that will result in constant growth in your love towards God.
7. We must learn to walk with God. In other words, follow His commands and obey Him. You need to be in a good place with God. This will please Him, and you'll be able to approach Him with confidence.

8. You need to get to know God intimately. This can happen because of the Holy Spirit dwelling in us. God is a spirit, and we need to approach Him in spirit and in truth. The Holy Spirit will help us to know God in an intimate and personal way through an understanding of the truth in God's word.

For the first seven years of my walk with the Lord, I used to wear a button that said, "I love Jesus" every single day. I never left the house without it. I was so happy with my newfound relationship with my God that I wanted everyone to know about the love of my life!

My prayer for you today is that you may glean some things from this book and use it to cultivate, improve and nurture your walk with the Lord. My main motivation for writing this book is so that everyone will love the Lord deeply. I hope you will learn to love God with your body, mind and soul. We need to be able to feel God's love for us. He is always pouring His love out on us. Being reassured of God's love for us will enable us to hold on until our eternal life with Him has come. Then we will be able to experience the full love of God.

In the next few chapters, I'm going to share with you some of my most personal interactions and experiences in my prayer closet with God.

CHAPTER 10

THE NECESSITY OF PRAYER

Eph 6:18 (NIV) says, *"And pray in the Spirit on all occasions with all kinds of prayers and requests..."*

We know that our main communication with God is accomplished through prayer. So, the question then is, what is prayer? When you talk to another person on earth, it's called having a conversation. When you talk to God, it's called prayer. It's who you are talking with that changes this special relationship. This prayer is much more than a conversation. It's an interaction with God with help from the Holy Spirit that puts you directly in touch with God immediately.

> *It's an interaction with God with help from the Holy Spirit that puts you directly in touch with God immediately.*

Romans 8:26 says, *"In the same way, the Spirit helps us in our weakness. We do not know what we ought to pray for, but the Spirit himself intercedes for us with groans that words cannot express."* (NIV)

To pray, you don't have to use your mouth or speak words if you don't want to. God makes it very easy for us to communicate with Him by thinking in your mind or by speaking out loud.

Jesus had an awesome prayer life. Luke 5:16 says, *"And he withdrew himself into the wilderness and prayed."* (NIV) Jesus knew what He was going to be facing here on earth, and He was in constant communication with His Father. I believe this is where He got the strength to face the very difficult task He was asked to do by His Father. Jesus knew that the way to communicate with His Father God was through prayer, and He set a good example for us to follow. Jesus even made sure that His disciples knew how to pray.

Matthew 6:9-13 says, *"After this manner therefore pray ye: Our Father which art in heaven, Hallowed be thy name. [10]Thy kingdom come, Thy will be done in earth, as it is in heaven. [11]Give us this day our daily bread. [12]And forgive us our debts, as we forgive our debtors. [13]And lead us not into temptation, but deliver us from evil: For thine is the kingdom, and the power, and the glory, forever. Amen"* (NIV)

This prayer is very special in that it contains a pattern of prayer that we should emulate the formula. It takes the guesswork out and gives us the proper things to say and the order in which to address God our Father. Let's try not to make prayer overly

> *Why should we pray? Because it's necessary to communicate with Him for our benefit.*

complicated or very formal. After you get used to praying like Jesus's example that He gave us, it will become second nature to you so that you say your own prayers to God.

So, why should we pray? Because it's necessary to communicate with Him for our benefit. We need to be in constant communication in order to not go off on our own agenda. Also, it keeps us being dependent on His grace and mercy so that we live with less fear and have peace of mind. God doesn't make us talk to Him. He has given us a free will and wants us to desire to talk to Him. He also doesn't need to hear from us because He's God, but we need to speak to Him and hear from Him. The real take away here is that we need Him for our daily spiritual survival. It's this constant communication and interaction with Him that keeps us full of hope and encouragement. He made us to need to depend on Him for everything. He is everything we need our Father God to be to us.

Something else for you to think about here is that the bible is very important in our relationship with God when you pray. It teaches us about Him, what He likes and what He doesn't like. It tells us what He will provide for us and, most importantly, how much He loves us. This love was made evident by the sacrifice of His Son, Jesus, by His death and resurrection. The Bible and the power of His Holy Spirit helps us to get a better understanding of who God is. This, in turn, helps us when we pray and bond with God. We need to have this intimate relationship with Him. He is a sensual God, and is emotionally connected to us.

He could have just created Adam from heaven, but He came to earth by the power of the Holy Spirit and created Adam from the dust of the earth, and then He Himself breathed into Adam. He covered Adam and Eve up with clothes when they had sinned. He showed parts of Himself to Moses. Do you see how intimate God can get with His creations? He has a long history of interacting with mankind. God wants to have a relationship with each and every one of us, and this is done through prayer and our constant interaction with Him.

CHAPTER 11

WHAT HAPPENS WHEN WE PRAY?

Let's examine the physical, mental and spiritual aspects of prayer. Jesus was very experienced in talking to His Father. He prayed often and hard.

Luke 22:44 says, *"And being in anguish, He prayed more earnestly, and His sweat was like drops of blood falling to the ground."* (NIV).

Now that is some heavy-duty praying to become so physically affected! Hannah, in the bible, prayed so hard that the priest thought she was drunk!

1 Samuel 1:13 says, *"Hannah was praying in her heart, and her lips were moving but her voice was not heard. Eli thought she was drunk."* (NIV).

I am going to draw from some of my own personal experiences about what happens when we pray. The reaction that happens to me depends on what I'm talking to God about. If I am praying about someone else's needs or a crisis's, I might be emotionally charged up and very intense as I ask God to help that person or about a situation. When I praise the Lord, I get very excited as I think of His goodness and all that He's done for me. If I'm meditating or being still in His presence, I feel relaxed and very mellow.

Worshiping God starts in my mind. It also affects me physically when singing and glorifying God. Praying affects me mentally. After I pray, I feel incredibly good. I have joy, love, hope, comfort, security, and I feel completely at peace. Any fear about my life is gone for a time. I say for a time because our mind forgets after a while, and other tests and trials come into our lives, so we again need to pray to be renewed daily, hourly, or if need be minute by minute. Ephesians 4:23 says, *"And be renewed in the spirit of your mind."* (NIV)

As you can see, a lot goes on inside of us, spiritually and physically when we pray to God. It's a whole body and mind experience! It's also a supernatural experience because it's not a human to human connection but a supernatural being to a human connection through a supernatural being called the Holy Spirit. Now that is something to really think about! I do that! It is what excites me and motivates me more to wanting to know God. I feel that it's an exciting thing to have a Father who is so far out of what we consider as normal. So, you can't expect to have a typical human to human relationship with Him. You must think out of the box. The bible is out of the box. Stretch yourself to accept and love God for who He is. He is far beyond your imagination, and anything can happen when we pray to Him. Let go of any

Worshiping God starts in our mind.

anxiety or fear and let God take you to a special place in your prayer times with Him.

CHAPTER 12

INTIMACY WITH GOD

James 4:8 says, *"Come near to God and He will come near to you."* (NIV).

Exactly what do I mean by the term intimacy with God? I believe it starts by knowing God. In the bible, we first learn about the word "know" in Genesis.

Genesis 4:1 ESV says, *"Now Adam knew Eve his wife, and she conceived and bore Cain, saying, "I have gotten a man with the help of the LORD."*

The term "knew" used in this verse was about Adam knowing his wife Eve physically. The word "know" used in the following scripture verse is also talking about a love connection:

John 17:3 says, *"Now this is eternal life: that they know you, the only true God, and Jesus Christ, whom you have sent."* (NIV).

How is it possible to have this kind of intimacy with God? Because of the following scripture verse, this does not seem humanly possible. John 4:24 says, *"God is spirit, and His worshipers must worship in the Spirit and in truth."* (NIV). But I tell you it is possible to know God not physically, but spiritually intimately.

> *I tell you it is possible to know God*
> *not physically, but spiritually*
> *intimately!*

Let's start with some basic advice about how to know God intimately:

1. Believe in Jesus Christ, repent from your sin and accept Jesus as your Lord and Savior.
2. Read the bible and study it.

3. Pray and talk to God your Father as often as you can off and on all day every day and in a private close the door and get alone with Him time of prayer.
4. Offer God your body as a living sacrifice. In other words, obey Him and follow His commands. Some examples of this action are Enoch, John the Baptist, Moses, Mary and Paul.
5. Live a life of holiness. Maintain a clean heart and repent if you've sinned. That also means be set apart from the world and love others as yourself.

After you have crossed these items off your checklist, now it's time to let go of any doubt and concern about the Holy Spirit, taking you on an intimate journey with the love of your life, God. This requires real private time with God when nobody else is around. The reason for this, for me, is that I usually cry out loud. I might also pray and sing out loud. There are times when I'm quiet before the Lord waiting on Him to speak to me. This type of prayer requires being alone in a quiet room so that I can concentrate on hearing God's voice.

There are times when I'm so in the spirit that I feel that I'm not even aware that I'm here on earth because I'm so caught up in the spirit of prayer! I feel like I'm safely hiding under the shadow of His wings, and it's a place that I don't want to ever leave. *It's when I'm in that place where I can really feel God's love for me.* I try hard to tell God how much I love Him, and that's when the tears begin to flow generously from my eyes. I pour my heart out to Him, but the words never really reveal just how deep my love is for Him because I'm human. So, as a result of this, I try to offer myself to God in obedience and service to Him. I feel this is the only way that I can let Him know that I truly love Him.

Now back to my prayer closet. I hope this chapter will help you to imagine your own path in developing your relationship to get closer to God!

Matthew 6:6 says, *"But when you pray, go into your room, close the door and pray to your Father, who is unseen. Then your Father, who sees what is done in secret, will reward you."* (NIV)

This verse is very important in establishing intimacy with God. It's definitely how I got to the point of being **OBSESSED WITH GOD!** Any relationship that you have with anybody *must be developed,* and developing a relationship with God is no different! Because we can't see Him, He has arranged other ways to get close to Him, and this is because of the third person in the Trinity, the Holy Spirit.

Another major thing is that you have got to want a deep *supernatural relationship* with God. This relationship is unlike anything that we are used to because it's with someone that we have never seen in person. For us humans, this is not the norm. I think many people might have difficulty letting go of what's normal and not be fearful or intimidated to love an invisible supernatural being who is God our Father.

There may be other times that we might go into deep prayer. When a crisis happens in a person's life, they might pray like they've never prayed before. They will see God as their Father, and they will cry and pray very hard. I'm sure they envision God on His throne, and they are at His feet begging Him for a miracle. That is *deep intimate prayer* also. So, we really do know how to pray passionately and deeply. We need to see God as not only the person we go to in a crisis but also in a loving personal relationship too. We need to approach Him in these times with as much passion.

I feel this is the most important chapter in my book. I want to leave you with King David's beautiful words of intimate passion for our wonderful God:

Psalm 63:1-8 says, *"O God, you are my God, earnestly I seek you; my soul thirsts for you, my body longs for you, in a dry and weary land where there is no water. I have seen you in the sanctuary and beheld your power and your glory. Because your love is better than life, my lips will glorify you. I will praise you as long as I live,* and in your name, I will lift up my hands. My soul will be satisfied as with the richest of foods; with singing lips, my mouth will praise you. On my bed I remember you; I think of you through the watches of the night. Because you are my help, I sing in the shadow of your wings. My soul clings to you; your right hand upholds me." (NIV).

CHAPTER 13

MY PERSONAL PRAYER SECRETS

When I became a committed Christian, I thought I didn't know how to pray. But in reality, I had been talking to God all along from my childhood into my adult life. I had always talked to Him like a friend. But when I became really committed to the Lord, I thought I had to be much more formal. I felt that I didn't know how to pray. So, I decided to start with Jesus's example of prayer that He gave the disciples, which was the Lord's prayer.

I prayed alone in my bedroom away from my husband and kids. I always pray lying down. I have suffered with a chronic illness and fatigue most of my life, so it was a better way for me to pray. I started out praying for about an hour, and then over time, I would pray for almost 6-8 hours a day 7 days a week! Some people thought it was quite odd to pray that long, but I had a lot to say to God, and He had a lot to say to me.

Many people wanted to know what I could be saying that took so long to pray. I first acknowledged who God was to me, just like it says in the Lord's prayer. Then I would have to say about *40 percent* of my prayer was telling God how much I loved Him. *30 percent* was me praying for people around the world to be saved. *20 percent* was God revealing Himself to me and *10 percent* asking God to answer my specific prayer needs. I would cry from the depths of my heart in intercession for others and then I would just tell God how much I loved Him to the point that I had no more energy after I prayed. During these prayer times, God would give me visions and messages. Everything always lined up with God's word. I shared all my experiences with my husband, and He would show me where it was in the bible.

I prayed for hours like this for about 20 years. My prayer life now is much more modified. I talk to God throughout my day, like talking to a friend and I have intimate private prayer about twice a week. My husband and I also pray for needs every day. The deep intercession prayer I just revealed to you about myself is not for everybody but intimate private prayer and talking to God off and on throughout your day *is for every single believer in Jesus Christ.* It keeps our relationship with God on a high-level, which Christians need for our spiritual survival.

You don't need to put pressure on yourself to have a big powerful prayer life right away. Start off with a few minutes a day and build on that. The main thing is to be hungry for more of God! We must desire to know everything about God our Father. Step away from seeing God as an old man with a long gray beard. *Don't keep God in a box and who you perceived Him to be like!* Open yourself to how He wants to reveal Himself to you. He is like an ever-flowing presence that will keep revealing Himself to you by the power of the Holy Spirit. The Holy Spirit lives inside of us upon salvation. He knows *everything* about God, and will reveal the deep things of God, which are mysteries of the kingdom of God.

> *The main thing is to be hungry for more of God!*

CHAPTER 14

PRAY UNTIL YOU CRY

Revelations 21:4 Says, *"He will wipe every tear from their eyes. There will be no more death or mourning or crying or pain, for the old order of things has passed away."* (NIV)

I cry a great deal when I pray. In fact, I cry for most of the time that I pray. Crying is associated with grief and pain. When I cry while praying, I find this is an emotional way of expressing my feelings to God. It connects me deeply with what I'm trying to emotionally convey to God. It's a way that I'm talking to God by pouring my heart out to Him. I have a saying that *"prayer ain't prayer till your nose starts a runnin'!"* As rough as this sounds to you, for me, this describes my prayer life. I must have a box of tissues with me when I pray.

> **When I pray, I see myself laying at God's feet and kissing them.**

I cry when I intercede for others in prayer, which is asking God to answer my prayers for the needs of other people. I also cry when I try to tell God how much I love Him and when I feel His presence! Expressing my love for Him takes up most of my time in prayer. I can't wait until the day when I see Him face to face, and I will be able to express my feelings to Him and worship Him in a close and perfect way. When I pray, I see myself laying at God's feet and kissing them. I know that when I get to heaven, I will be able to connect with God intimately on His level. I can hardly wait, but until then, I will continue to cry and pray like this kind of prayer:

Dear God, my Precious Father,

I'm so glad that you're going to wipe every tear away from my eyes one day, but I don't want all my tears wiped away. I do want you to wipe the bad tears away, which are the ones that came from my earthly suffering. *But there are some special tears that I hope you've collected and will never get rid of, and they are my tears of love for you!* My God, I love you so very much, and in my times of prayer, I have cried so hard because of my love for you.

My wonderful, merciful and caring God accept my good tears. Every tear of love I shed for you is from deep within my heart. My heart aches for You, and each tear represents the depths of that love.

Please don't wipe away my liquid signs of love for You from my eyes. How else will I be able to tell you how much I love You? Is there a way? Can I pour out my oil on You? Can I too, wash Your

> *Please don't wipe away my liquid signs of love for You from my eyes.*

feet with my hair? I know You are a spirit so how can I pour my love out on You my Precious Father? My tears, my tears, my tears are for You!

Luke 7:38 says, *"And as she stood behind Him at His feet weeping, she began to wet His feet with her tears. Then she wiped them with her hair, kissed them and poured perfume on them."* (NIV).

Please help me Holy Spirit to worship my Father, and I will be so happy. Father God, when I get to heaven, will I be able to lay before Your throne to express my adoration for all the love that You have shown me?

Psalms 99:5 says, *"Exalt the LORD our God and worship at His footstool; He is holy."* (NIV).

I think a lot about what I will do when I am finally in Your presence. I'm going to want to hug You tightly and say thank You for making me, forgiving me, saving me, loving me and accepting me, warts and all! Yes, these tears God, that I have on my face right now, they are for You! Please don't wipe my love away!

God, there are no words in my mouth, only my tears of love, my human expression of passion for You. My tears are my worship, Father. Please don't wipe my tears away! You've given me so much, and my good tears are all I have to give You. They are symbolic of my heart's cry of worship and praise to You!

Will I remember these times of prayer and intimate fellowship with You? They are so precious to me! Will my love for You be lost in the history of my earthly existence? I realize that I'm asking so many questions. I don't want my good tears to be gone from my memory of my prayer experiences with You. I cherish my good tears and these times of being close to You.

I know when I get to heaven, you'll be waiting for me, and I'll have a glorified body. I'll be like You and our relationship will be on a different level! But I want to say this, while I'm still down here, please don't wipe my good tears away. They are my joy, my happiness, and my love that I have for You! I love you so!!

From Your daughter filled with my good tears for You,

Tanya

CHAPTER 15

WORSHIP NOW FOR

HEAVEN'S SAKE

One morning while I was in my prayer closet fellowshipping with the God, I asked, "Him how I will worship You in heaven?" He said that I'll have a whole different kind of relationship with Him

> *In my prayer closet, I give myself over*
> *to worshiping God as passionately and*
> *as deeply as I can.*

than I have now! He said I'll be transformed and that I will be able to relate to Him on an incredibly higher mental, physical and spiritual level! I'm really looking forward to that!

Philippians 3:20-21 says, *"But our citizenship is in heaven. And we eagerly await a Savior from there, the Lord Jesus Christ, 21 who, by the power that enables him to bring everything under his control, will transform our lowly bodies so that they will be like his glorious body."* (NIV)

The bible says I'll have a glorious body! Praise the Lord! I'll be transformed into something very different from what I am now.

God told me that because of my new state of being that my worship and praise to Him will be perfect. He said that He can't tell me anymore than that because it's not for me to know now. I am happy just knowing that I will be able to worship God perfectly one day!

In my prayer closet, *I give myself over to worshiping God as passionately and as deeply as I can!* I pour my worship out on Him. I tell God all the time that I worship the ground He walks on. I envision myself at the foot of His throne, hugging His feet!

I'm a soloist, and when I sing my songs, I sing them with everything that I have in me. I know when people see me sing, they might be thinking, "that woman is very emotional when she sings!" Singing about God is total worship for me. I sometimes forget that there are people watching me because I'm so into worshipping the Lord in song. There is something about worshipping God that uniquely connects us to Him, and I take full advantage of that.

Our heavenly worship will be so incredible! We'll see Him face to face, and our entire being will be connected to God in the most profound way. It will be on a level that we just can't even imagine! We'll finally be able to experience all of His awesomeness and one hundred percent of God. Can you imagine receiving all the love that God ever had for us and then worshipping Him knowing this pure love? I think it will take an eternity to worship God.

One other aspect about God that will be the most amazing thing ever will be that we will be able to completely understand the Trinity, and we will be able to worship the Father, Son and Holy Spirit all together!

We have this awesome opportunity to let God know just how much we really love Him by worshipping Him passionately right now. We might even worship Him to the point of becoming **OBSESSED** with Him. You know, like He is constantly on our mind.

So as far as me wanting to know how I will worship Him in heaven, I'll have to wait until I get there to do that! But for right now, I will worship God the earthly way, with my body, soul, mind, voice, with all my strength, with all my heart and in prayer.

CHAPTER 16
HOW TO PRAYERFULLY
WORSHIP GOD

To get a glimpse of God and to fully understand prayerful worship is this, *it's to know God from the knowledge that you have gleaned about Him from the bible.* But It isn't until you have worshiped God in the secret place of the most high that you can truly experience the mental, physical and emotional relationship with God. This kind of worshipful prayer, along with the intense

> *This type of prayer is different. It involves not only thinking about and speaking to God but moving into a very deep spiritual connection with Him.*

presence of the Holy Spirit, allows us to have a very intimate relationship with God our Father.

This type of prayer is different from all other kinds of prayer. It involves not only thinking about and speaking to God but *moving into a very deep spiritual connection with Him.* This allows you to feel God's presence to the point that you forget about yourself and everything around you. It's just you and God! This kind of prayer makes you want to cry your heart out for your love for Him. You may even want to lie on the floor, face down to worship Him. At this point in your prayer, you may want to be very still and let the Holy Spirit help you to be one with God supernaturally. You might even feel like you are in a trance. God will be ministering to you and speaking to you. He could give you a vision or give you a song that you know or one you never heard of before. You will experience the Glory of God during this time and feel like nothing in the world can harm you during this kind of prayer. You will feel so safe. You will feel extreme love from Him and will feel very relaxed in your spirit.

To pray and worship God this way, you need to get *ALONE* with Him. It would be great if nobody was home or that you could at least be alone in a room. This is a very special time just with you and God. Some people may feel uncomfortable praying this way, and I can understand that. But this relationship supersedes all other relationships, and if one can be intimate with their husband, this relationship truly surpasses even that. This is our God, the Supreme Being in the universe, creator of everything and ruler over all things, and He is so in love with me and you! We might

> ## *IT'S ALL ABOUT HIM!!!! HE IS EVERYTHING!!! WE OWE HIM EVERYTHING!!!!*

not comprehend His full unique majesty. But we can get a small glimpse of it and have supernatural experiences with Him when we get into our secret prayer closet.

So why am I telling you all about my very personal prayer experiences? Because I want you to experience God like I have! I'm not special...I just love God so very much, and I open myself up to Him! *I let go and let God have His way with me!* I told God a long time ago that I want to know and experience everything thing that a human being can possibly experience with Him. There used to be a TV commercial for a bathwater softener that said, "Calgon... take me away!"

I've said that to the Lord.... *"Lord... take me away!"* Tell me everything and show me everything about Yourself that I can humanly handle.

This life, our world, our existence is *ALL ABOUT HIM!!!!*

HE IS EVERYTHING!!! WE OWE HIM EVERYTHING!!!! None of these things down here on earth is as important as He is!!! We just don't always remember or can't grasp the fact that this is not our home...we are passing through on our way to the greatest thing that will ever happen to us.... eternal life with our God!!!!

Just thinking about who God is and what He's done for us makes me want to cry out from the depths of my heart, "I love you, God!!!" Thank you, Jesus!!! We can't even thank Him enough. All we can do is cry out of our love and appreciation for Him. We need to live our lives for Him so that we can bring glory to His Holy name.

I want to worship God in the deepest way that I can. The more I worship God, the less afraid I feel about getting through this difficult journey of life. I feel the Holy Spirit is leading me to write this. I am stepping out on a limb with this message because it's extremely personal, but I feel led to give it.

The cure and the answer for the Church, which is you and I, is to *love God very deeply!* We should humble ourselves and worship the Lord. We need to love Him from deep inside our hearts. Stop all the busyness. All the running all over the place. We need to get off cell phones, turn off the TV's, cut back on all the extra activities and get to the secret place of prayer, and worship the Lord your God! Time is running out for our only opportunity forever to love God this way in our mortal form. Catastrophes are happening so fast and furious that nobody is promised one more day of life. *We must seek God and get others to seek God with all their heart.*

This Supernatural Being is our God and Father. We should, in our mind and heart, be on our face before Him, bowed down in a very humbled position. We are God's humble servants, and we should be serving and worshipping Him here on earth because it is also what we will be doing in heaven. Every knee will bow to God, but who is willing to do this now? These acts of humility will impress God the most now because we have never seen Him face to face, but even so, we have believed what the bible says about Him. *Oh, people of God, let's worship Him now!*

In the days to come, we really need to be aware of what the bible says about what will happen in the last days. We all see the signs, and we all sense that something is going on in our world. All eyes should be focused on God. I feel an urgency today like I've never felt before. We should all be saying this. Oh Lord, my God, I do so worship you! I bow before you and give you all the honor and praise that You deserve!

"Dear Lord, help us to see the seriousness of the times and help us to know how much we need to worship You! Holy Spirit help us in our worship to God. Help us to have a humble servant's heart and attitude. Help us to completely let go in our secret prayer closet and get into that place of deep worship. Thank you for all you've done and will do for us, in Jesus's name ...Amen."

God rewards those who diligently seek Him or, in other words, sincerely or earnestly look for Him!

CHAPTER 17

HOW TO SEE GOD'S FACE

Psalms 27:8 says, *"My heart says of you, "Seek his face!" Your face, LORD, I will seek."* Exodus 33:20 says, *"But, He said, "you cannot see My face, for no one may see Me and live."* (NIV). Before you say, "Ok, she has gone too far because nobody can see God's face and live!" give me a chance to explain.

The bible is very clear that we *can't* see God's face and live. Why? Because we have a sinful nature and God is holy. And finally, because God is a spirit. You might say, "that's no reason not to see God because we have a spirit inside of us too." Our spirit is contained in a human body, so we can't see God's face because seeing God requires the death of our mortal body. The bible reveals some interesting facts about what God is like. Here's one example.

Revelation 21:23 says, *"The city does not need the sun or the moon to shine on it, for the glory of God gives it light, and the Lamb is its lamp."* (NIV). But," he said, "you cannot see my face, for no one may see me and live." God is brighter than the sun. He is so bright that if we saw Him in His Holy form, we would burn up in immediately!

We can't even imagine how bright and radiant the Glory of God is! Our human mind just can't comprehend this! God's real-life form and His Holiness is too awesome for a human being to be able to withstand it.

> *God's real-life form and His Holiness are too awesome for a human being to be able to withstand it.*

That's why we have to wait until our bodies have changed forms to a glorified body after we die, to see Him as He really is.

Now God has made some special up close and personal revelations of Himself to a few humans like appearing to Adam and Eve and Moses. He was able to transform Himself into a different form so that He could communicate with people on a personal level here on earth.

So how can we see God's face? One day I was watching Little House on the Prairie and Laura's sister Mary, who was blind, had met a man she would later marry. Before they had their first kiss, they wanted to know what each other looked like, so they took turns running their fingers over each other's face.

Knowing God is like that, if you run your fingers over His face, you will see God. I have seen God, not face to face or in His natural form, but in the spirit. We must experience Him in the spirit if we want to know Him intimately.

John 4:24 says, *"God is spirit, and His worshipers must worship in the Spirit and in truth."* (NIV)

How can you experience God?

1. You must be born again, saved, a child of God, and a Christian.
2. You need to know what the bible says about Him and His nature.
3. You need to pray to Him.
4. You need to have fellowship with Him.
5. You must learn to hear His voice.
6. You need to meditate, be still and wait in His presence.
7. You should be able to feel His love for you and respond back to Him.
8. You should meet Him in the secret place, which is your prayer closet.
9. You should devote time to this, not a few minutes but some uninterrupted time alone with Him.
10. You should be able to laugh, cry, and reveal your heart to Him.
11. You should be able to let Him minister to you, and you minister to Him.

12. You should give yourself over to the Holy Spirit and let Him lead you into your time of prayer and devotion to God.
13. You should submit and surrender all fear and anxiety about going deep in God. Let go and let God in!
14. You should trust Him with your heart, mind, and soul
15. Love Him with your mind, spirit, and body.
16. You should ask Him to search your heart and be clean before Him. Repent of any sins and unforgiveness.
17. You should now wait for His Shekinah to touch you. Then reach out and rub your fingers over His face in your mind, and you will experience His glorious features in your spirit.

I have experienced this myself many times over the years. As I write this chapter, the tears are welling up in my eyes because I'm remembering how very beautiful God is. I don't think we realize that God could be so beautiful. His beauty takes my breath away. I've never seen such beauty like that in my whole life. I felt the glow of His beauty on my hands. This is an amazing thing, but when you experience the *Shekinah Glory of God*, it takes away any fear you may have. I felt like nothing could touch me or hurt me. I had so much peace during this time of prayer.

I never want the manifestation of His presence to stop. Then the beauty of that moment fades into the passing hours until it's just a wonderful memory. *The knowledge of what God's word says He is as confirmed by the Holy Spirit stays in my heart and mind long after.*

God doesn't let us stay in His Shekinah Glory. Therefore, we must pray often because we, as humans, can't maintain that part of the relationship every day like that. It's like staying up on the mountain top. Growth happens in the valley.

We need these kinds of visitations with the Lord because it further develops our relationship with Him. When the difficulties of life beat us down, we have the memories of our experiences with Him. This establishes a close relationship with our Father God, and it keeps us steady to the point that we can say that our spirit is so satisfied.

We need these kinds of visitations with the Lord because it further develops our relationship with Him.

Psalms 63:5-6 says, *"I will be fully satisfied as with the richest of foods; with singing lips my mouth will praise You. On my bed I remember You; I think of You through the watches of the night."* (NIV)

CHAPTER 18

KISSING JESUS FEET

Luke 7:37-38 says, *"A woman in that town who lived a sinful life learned that Jesus was eating at the Pharisee's house, so she came there with an alabaster jar of perfume. 38 As she stood behind him at his feet weeping, she began to wet his feet with her tears. Then she wiped them with her hair, kissed them and poured perfume on them."* (NIV) The most expensive perfume in the world is by Clive Christian's Imperial Majesty: with a price tag of

> *Jesus was there through everything that I had been through in my life!*

$215,000. The most expensive perfume I know of is the one that was poured out of my heart for my Lord and Savior Jesus Christ. The cost of it was very high!

I can't speak about the woman in the story that's found in the scripture. I wasn't there. But I can share about my oil for my Lord and Savior.

Matthew 26:7 says, *"a woman came to Him with an alabaster jar of very expensive perfume, which she poured on His head as He was reclining at the table."* (NIV) If someone is reading this today and you heard about this Jesus but don't believe He is real, then read my story:

I've had two visions that have impacted me in a special way. The first one happened years ago at the beginning of my Christian walk. I was feeling like Jesus wasn't taking care of me. I had repented of my sins and made Jesus my Lord and Savior, but I felt that Jesus was not moving fast enough, answering my prayers. I felt I had suffered a lot in the past, but where was He now? I was pretty much acting like a baby Christian. Whine, whine, whine!

One day when I was deep in prayer, and as I had my eyes closed, I saw my life as if I were watching TV. Jesus showed me all the times that He was there for me, guiding me and protecting me. I saw many scenes of my life that I had forgotten. Jesus was there through everything that I had been through in my life! After seeing this vision, I cried so hard I could barely breathe. This was the beginning of me saving up for my expensive oil.

The second vision was about the love of Jesus. I can tell you that I have never experienced that amount of love in my life! This experience was like a near-death experience. I experienced a microsecond of the incredible pure love of Jesus that we

> *I'm not God's enemy anymore, I'm His child, and my heart is running over with this oil!*

will know and feel after we die. It was His love combined with peace, happiness, joy, contentment, safety, and comfort all rolled into one! It was an extremely intense feeling. Just writing about this is bringing tears to my eyes. *Jesus has touched me like no other!!!!!!!!* I now have my alabaster jar full of oil.

Now about my oil. Ever since these two visions, I have been through some difficult trials, and the oil that I have in my heart has built up because of seeing how the Lord has always been there for me. God has given me victory time and time again! Because of the many hours I have been in prayer, God revealed Himself to me and has shown me so much love! But the main reason for my oil is because the older I get, the more I understand how wicked my heart really is. I know His truth and holiness well now through studying the bible and prayer. I understand who my God is and the sacrifice His only Son made for me. Knowing this about my Lord causes the oil to builds up in me! I'm not God's enemy anymore, *I'm His child, and my heart is running over with this oil!*

My Prayer secret is this; when I get into my deep my prayer with God, I spend *MOST* of my time telling the Lord how much I love Him. I pray other things too, but mainly it's worshipping Him. When I get into the throne room, I get on my face before my very Holy God, and I crawl up to Him and kiss His feet. I can pray that way for hours. There is no way except in my obedience to God to express my love in a human way. God, who is a spirit, must be worshipped in spirit and in truth. It's because of His Holy Spirit who lives in me that I CAN have this relationship with God this way.

I admire the woman in the bible with the alabaster jar. I know that Jesus is not here on earth, and I cannot anoint Him the way that she did. But when we believe in Jesus and accept Him into our lives, the Holy Spirit at that moment comes and *LIVES IN US!* This is so awesome! Because of Him, we can be connected to God. Now we can worship Him, and we can pour that very expensive oil on Him too.

Side note: I would like you to listen to a song on this subject by CeCe Winans called *Alabaster Box* before you read the next chapter. Have some tissues ready. This song can really usher you into some serious worship.

CHAPTER 19

PROSKUNEO IS GREAT FOR PRAYER

One day I was praying, I had a very unusual experience. I felt the presence of the Lord come over me. I also kept hearing a word in my heart and mind. This word was familiar to me, and the word was *Proskuneo* (pros-koo-neh'-o).

During this awesome time of prayer, I felt like I could just enjoy this unusual feeling of His presence forever. I was breathless because I was experiencing God's unique ability to reveal Himself to me in this way. I was totally speechless because of the awe of it all. Most of all, I kept thinking to myself how real God is and how I'm so grateful to be His child!

> *Proskuneo is a form of worship. It means to kiss like a dog licking his owners' hands.*

Psalms 95:6 says, *"Come, let us bow down in worship, let us kneel before the LORD our Maker."*

Proskuneo is a form of worship. It means to *kiss like a dog licking his owners' hands.* This is surely a very intimate way of showing great admiration to someone. It also means to bow or to fall down before someone of special significance or to lay prostrate in front of someone in total reverence to them. It's a way of expressing total respect and is a posture of humility to an admired person.

Why did God show me this? Because I'm so hungry for more of God, and I desire to see Him and know Him all the time. I've been seeking Him a lot lately. I want to spend the rest of my life passionately seeking Him even more. I desperately want for those who don't know Him in a deeply to know Him more intimately.

Proskuneo is a type of worship that I do in my worship to my Father God. I've been worshipping Him this way for all my committed Christian life! I don't know any other way to worship Him. It's my way of knowing God, fellowshipping with Him, and ministering to Him personally. *I recognize His holiness, and I understand who He is to me. He's Holy, He's is supernatural, He's my creator, He owns me, and He loves me so!* This knowledge makes me want to Proskuneo Him.

Proskuneo is a word that may sound a little strange...but it's a word that should be in our spiritual vocabulary and in our heart and mind when it comes to our adoration and interaction with God. I really don't know of any other way of expressing humbling admiration for God other than *Proskuneo.*

> *I recognize His holiness, and I understand who He is to me. He's Holy, He's is supernatural, He's my creator, He owns me, and He loves me so!*

People kiss the Pope's ring and bow before a King and Queen. People fall out before great entertainers at a concert. Remember the crowd's response to the Beatles and Michael Jackson? *How much greater is God the Father, God the Son and God the Holy Ghost?* In your mind, when you pray, you should see yourself *bowing* down to God this way. Some people lay prostrate on the floor when they pray. Whatever it takes for you to worship God! Anything that will help you to humble yourself and worship our Almighty God, do it.

CHAPTER 20

WHEN YOU REALLY SEE GOD

I would like to start this chapter with two quotes from Rev. A.W. Tozer (1897-1963) from his book, *The Knowledge of the Holy*[1], which speaks about our relationship with God. *"What comes into our minds when we think about God is the most important thing about us,"* *"If what we conceive God to be, He is not, how then shall we think of Him?"* These questions will really expose what we think about our Father God.

What do you think about your earthly father? Some fathers may not have been in their child's life. Some fathers may have been in their child's life but were distant, or their father had issues that caused much heartache to their child. Some fathers may have even been a great dad. What do you think about your Father, who is your creator and the creator of the entire universe? Do you really get who He is? Do you understand Him at all?

There was a movie that came out in 2009 called *Avatar.* It was a big hit and quite unique because it had half-human and half animated characters. The movie was very touching and heartfelt to me. One of the main character's names was *Neytiri,* who didn't like the other lead character named *Jake Sully* at first. As she developed a relationship with him, she told him one day, *"I see you!"* which means she really understood him. I believe she experienced the heart of Jake in who she eventually grew to know and fall in love with.

One day when I was deep in my private prayer closet with God, and I was feeling His presence in a powerful way, I just kept crying out to the Lord, "I see you; I see you"! I was crying so hard, and I was very emotional because I felt the essence of who He is in that moment. I can't explain to you in words what I felt, but in my heart, I experienced Him. All that the bible said that God is, I felt at that moment.

---

[1] *The Knowledge of the Holy,* (1961) New York: Harper & Row, ISBN 0-06-068412-7 (New edition: Cross Reach Publications)

God gives us a great description of *His creativity* in Genesis. He gives us a great description of *His powerful attributes* in the book of Job. He also gives us a beautiful description of *His love for mankind* in the book of John. And then finally, a glimpse of *His glorious majesty* in the book of Revelations. *Do you see Him?*

> *I just kept crying out to the Lord, "I see you; I see you"!*

There is a very familiar Scripture verse in the bible that really says something about God's heart that makes me cry. John 3:16 says, *"For God so loved the world, that He gave His only begotten Son, that whosoever believeth in Him should not perish, but have everlasting life."* (KJV).

The thing that has affected me so much is a two-letter word in the verse, which is *"so."* That two-letter word penetrates all the way down into my heart! That word "so" is for me and for you. *God so loves me!* So means a whole lot to me!
The word so, in this verse, covers me with everything I need as a human being! It covers all the love that I have ever looked for! That word *so*, pulls me up when I'm down, lonely, sick or scared. *Do you see Him?*

> *That two-letter word penetrates all the way down into my heart! That word "so" is for me and for you. God so loves me!*

Please try to experience and know God in your own way. You need to do this if you, too, want to become *"OBSESSED WITH GOD!"* Jeremiah 9:24 says, *"but let the one who boasts boast about this: that they have the understanding to know Me, that I am the LORD, who exercises kindness, justice and righteousness on earth, for in these I delight," declares the LORD."* (NIV)

CHAPTER 21
MY OBSESSION WITH GOD

My *OBSESSION* with God began in 1983 when God healed me miraculously of depression and suicidal ideations. *God won me over, and the OBSESSION was on!* The following two scriptures have changed my life!!!

When Jesus was here on earth, He instructed the disciples to do this: Luke 10:27 says, *"He answered, "Love the Lord your God with all your heart and with all your soul and with all your strength and with all your mind'; and, 'Love your neighbor as yourself.'"* 1 Corinthians 2:10 says, *"these are the things God has revealed to us by His Spirit. The Spirit searches all things, even the deep things of God."* (NIV)

I interpreted this as *love God like crazy,* and the Holy Spirit can tell you deep things of God! *I wanted to know everything I could know about God, who had just miraculously healed me and let me feel His love!* I wanted to love Him as intensely as I could. I planned to accomplish by praying to Him and by serving Him. My *mission* is to *share* the good news of Jesus Christ with others.

> *love God like crazy, and the Holy*
> *Spirit can tell you deep things of God!*

I must admit some people have found me intense and a little strange, but I'm OK with that! *It's who I am now!* I always try to not cross the line because God would never want me to misrepresent Him by behaving off the charts. *I'm just a little...intense!*

I know that God is real, loving and kind. So, my goal is to let others know about His goodness and His wonderful plan for their lives. How can I possibly keep this great information to myself? *I haven't, and I won't!*

Does this love thing that God and I have going keep me from experiencing trials and suffering? *No, it doesn't!* But I try to keep trials in their place in my life, and I keep them separate from my love for God. I try to love Him just because of who He is. He helps me to get through my trials, and I even get upset sometimes if He does not answer my prayers the way I want or fast enough! But I love Him anyway! I mention this here because many times, it's so easy to be mad at God, and our love for Him can decline, and I tell you that is not good for us. This is the time when we need Him the most. His love for us never declines, but ours can because we are human.

> *God's perfect love will help us in times of difficulty!*

We must learn to keep our intimate relationship at a peak level because doubt and fear will come over us and pull us down. This verse makes me want to cry good tears: 1 John 4:18 says, *"There is no fear in love. But perfect love drives out fear because fear has to do with punishment. The one who fears is not made perfect in love."* (NIV) *God's perfect love will help us in times of difficulty!*

It holds us up and helps us to be strong in Him. God's love is powerful!

Yes, I am **OBSESSED WITH GOD!** *I'm emotionally addicted to His love for me!* One day I'm going to be able to experience His pure love for me, but until then, I will have to be thirsty for Him. This thirst can only be satisfied by prayer, learning about Him from bible study, worshipping Him, and by the power of the Holy Spirit.

CHAPTER 22

WHAT WILL YOU DO NOW?

I have poured my heart out and have shared some of my most personal prayer secrets. I've tried to explain how much God loves you and how His love for us started. As I have stated, our relationship with God, is something that has to be developed over time. The important thing here is not to look back at your shortcomings in your desire to be closer to God. Start today building a new foundation and going forward. God doesn't *need* our love. He is self-sufficient. *But we need to know and feel His love! This comes by experiencing Him through prayer, knowing the bible, and with the help from Holy Spirit.* Even going through trials can reveal God's love for us when we see the miracles that happen when He helps us through them.

> *He is self-sufficient. But we need to know and feel His love! This comes by experiencing Him through prayer, knowing the bible, and with the help from Holy Spirit!*

Every miracle and victory that God blesses us with will show His love for us. Some people find it very difficult to sense or feel Gods' love for them. They may have experienced great pain in their life as a child or have had some traumatic experience that caused them to be angry with God. But after you've accepted Jesus Christ as your Lord and Savior, the Holy Spirit starts to confirm what you have heard and read from the bible, and God's love for you will become more apparent.

I want to just say to you, *please believe that God loves you so much!* I know my mere words can't make you love Him more. It's a process. I didn't love my husband passionately from the first day I met Him. I grew to know and love him through a process called dating or our courtship. Over time our love grew, and we got married.

> *I'm no different than you. We are all special to God! He is available to all of us!*

Be patient with yourself! Even if you struggle with your love for God, keep trying to move forward! You will be rewarded with so much love, joy and peace. Even if the bad times do come, you won't faint. *You will be confident that your Father God will see you through!* There are real advantages of being assured of God's love for you.

For those that are reading this and have never asked Jesus for forgiveness and you never repented from your sins, please ask God to forgive you and ask Him to be the Lord of your life. Your life will be changed forever. Romans 10:9 says, *"If you declare with your mouth, 'Jesus is Lord,' and believe in your heart that God raised Him from the dead, you will be saved.* (NIV).

If you are a Christian, why not recommit yourself to know God better. 1 John 4:16 says, *"And so we know and rely on the love God has for us. God is love. Whoever lives in love lives in God and God in them."* (NIV).

Finally, I'm no different than you. *We are all special to God!* He is available to all of us. This scripture explains my craving for *more of God:*

Psalms 63:1 says, *"You, God, are my God, earnestly I seek you; I thirst for you, my whole being longs for you, in a dry and parched land where there is no water."* (NIV).
This scripture explains why I took Jesus' words that He commanded very seriously, which led to my **OBSESSION:**

Deuteronomy 10:12 says, *"And now, Israel, what does the LORD your God ask of you but to fear the LORD your God, to walk in obedience to Him, to love Him, to serve the LORD your God with all your heart and with all your soul"* (NIV)

CHAPTER 23

THE CHALLENGE

I'm sure you have read many books on all kinds of topics from the bible. You may not have read one on being obsessed with God, but I'm asking you to *give my book some thought*. The subtitle for my book is called *"Intimacy with God."* When you think of this subtitle, I think it really explains what can happen when you become **OBSESSED WITH GOD!**

I challenge everyone who reads this book to go on a mission to become **OBSESSED WITH GOD.** Dig into the scriptures and study and find out everything that God has allowed you to know about Himself. There is a lot of information too! *Set some real private time to be alone with God in prayer!* Then tell yourself to let go of any hesitation you might have about letting the Holy Spirit reveal God to you. Open yourself up to Him. *Talk to Him*, use the Lord's prayer like I told you as a model addressing God as your Father. Praise Him, worship Him, thank Him, share your concerns, listen for His voice, and, most of all, love on Him.

> *Praise Him, worship Him, thank Him, share your concerns, listen for His voice, and, most of all, love on Him!*

I know that all this might sound very personal to you, but this is what is needed to be really close to God. I want to share with you how I taught my kids to hear God's voice. *God will always tell you that He loves you when you seek Him!* I told my kids close their eyes, and I said for them to, *tell God you love Him and wait for Him to tell you back that He loves you too.* He always answers you and will tell you that He loves you too. We may not be able to see God face to face, but I tell you, you can hear Him talk to you!

John 10:27 says, *"My sheep listen to my voice; I know them, and they follow me."* (NIV)

I really hope this book will help you on your journey to a deeper and more intimate relationship with God.

Dear Father God, I pray that everyone who reads this book has repented from their sin and has asked your Son Jesus to be their Lord and Savior. I also pray they will desire to become intimate with you. I also pray they will know you in a more profound way that will reinforce your love for them in their heart. I ask this in Jesus's name Amen.

God bless you all on your journey to become OBSESSED WITH GOD!

Love,

Tanya